BARACK
OBAMA

★ United States President ★

Updated and expanded!

GROSSET & DUNLAP
Published by the Penguin Group
Penguin Group (USA) Inc., 375 Hudson Street, New York, New York 10014, USA
Penguin Group (Canada), 90 Eglinton Avenue East, Suite 700, Toronto,
Ontario M4P 2Y3, Canada
(a division of Pearson Penguin Canada Inc.)
Penguin Books Ltd., 80 Strand, London WC2R 0RL, England
Penguin Group Ireland, 25 St. Stephen's Green, Dublin 2, Ireland
(a division of Penguin Books Ltd.)
Penguin Group (Australia), 250 Camberwell Road, Camberwell, Victoria 3124, Australia
(a division of Pearson Australia Group Pty. Ltd.)
Penguin Books India Pvt. Ltd., 11 Community Centre, Panchsheel Park,
New Delhi—110 017, India
Penguin Group (NZ), 67 Apollo Drive, Rosedale, North Shore 0632, New Zealand
(a division of Pearson New Zealand Ltd.)
Penguin Books (South Africa) (Pty.) Ltd., 24 Sturdee Avenue,
Rosebank, Johannesburg 2196, South Africa

Penguin Books Ltd., Registered Offices: 80 Strand, London WC2R 0RL, England

Photo Credits: cover: © Associated Press, © Alice Scully/iStockphoto (background); title page:
© Jason Reed/Reuters/Corbis; pages 1-2: © Associated Press; pages 4-5: © Associated Press;
pages 6-7: © Associated Press; page 15: © Barackobama.com; page 17: © Remi Salette/
Corbis Sygma; pages 18-19: © Associated Press; page 27: © Steve Liss/Time Life Pictures/Getty
Images; page 31: © Barackobama.com; page 33: © Ryan McVay/Photodisc; page 36:
© Associated Press; page 37: © Getty Images; page 39: © Kevin LaMarque/Reuters/Corbis;
pages 40-41: © Getty Images; page 43: © Associated Press; page 44: © Associated Press;
page 45: © Associated Press (top photo), © Associated Press (bottom photo); page 46:
© Associated Press; page 47: © Associated Press; page 48: © Getty Images; page 49:
© Associated Press; page 50: © Grosset & Dunlap; page 51: © Associated Press; pages 52-53: ©
Associated Press; page 54: © Getty Images; page 55: © Getty Images; page 56:
© Getty Images; page 57: © AFP/Getty Images; page 61: © Associated Press; page 64:
© Associated Press

Originally published in 2008 as *Barack Obama: An American Story*.

Library of Congress Control Number: 2008049764

ISBN 978-0-448-45234-0   10 9 8 7 6 5 4 3 2 1

BARACK
OBAMA
★ United States President ★

Updated and expanded!

By Roberta Edwards

Illustrated by Ken Call
and with photographs

Grosset & Dunlap

February 23, 2007

A huge crowd has gathered in Austin, Texas. About twenty thousand people are here, all hoping to see one man. Are they waiting for a rock star? Or a famous

movie actor? Or a sports legend?

No. The crowd has come to hear Senator Barack Obama speak. (You say his name like this: buh-ROCK oh-BAH-ma.)

He is tall—six feet, two inches—and thin. He has a wide, friendly smile. He looks much younger than forty-five years old.

Only three years earlier, in 2004, he was elected to the U.S. Senate from the state of Illinois. Now he has an even bigger dream: He wants to be the first African American to become president of the United States. Today, when someone hands him a cowboy hat, he puts it on right away.

He's in Texas, after all.

Not so long ago, people would hear the name Barack Obama and say, "Who?" They'd get his name all mixed up. He said he was sometimes called "Barack Yo Mama" or "Barack Alabama."

The name Barack means "blessed." And indeed, Barack Obama is blessed in many ways. He is smart and talented and confident. He has a wonderful family. And he has a way of making people, even total strangers, listen.

But growing up, Barack did not always feel blessed. He felt different. He lived with his mom and her parents. They were white. His dad, who was black, lived far away in Africa.

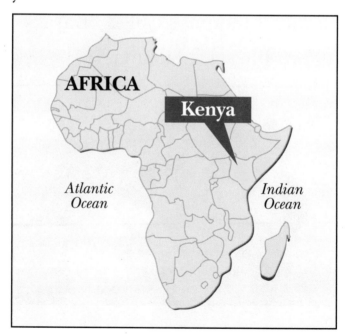

His father's name was also Barack Obama. Barack Sr. came from a tiny village in Kenya, a country on the east coast of Africa. His school was in a shack with a tin roof. His family belonged to the Luo tribe. They herded goats in the boiling sun. But Barack Sr. wanted a different life. He wanted to go to college. He was selected by government leaders to attend a university in the United States— the University of Hawaii.

Barack's mother, Ann Dunham, was born thousands of miles away from Kenya, across an ocean on a different continent.

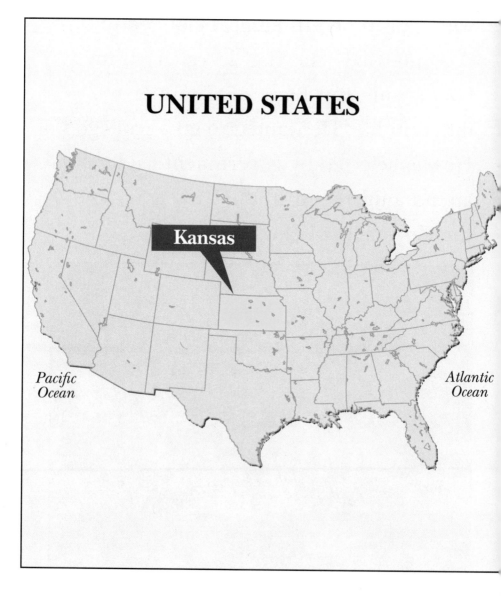

UNITED STATES

Kansas

Pacific
Ocean

Atlantic
Ocean

Ann grew up in a small town in Kansas. Her father worked on oil rigs and did farmwork. Her mother worked at a bank.

It is hard to imagine two places more different than Kansas and Kenya.

Barack's parents met when they were
both students at the University of Hawaii.
His father was twenty-three years old. His
mother was eighteen, a first-year student.
They fell in love and got married. This was
a time when there were very few marriages
between white people and black people.
Ann's parents, however, accepted their new
son-in-law.

Baby Barack was born in Honolulu,
Hawaii, on August 4, 1961.

But, sadly, the marriage did not last
long. Little Barack was only two years old
when his parents separated. Eventually
his father moved back to Africa.

Most of what Barack knew about his
father came from family photographs,
from the letters he received, and from the
stories his mother told.

Barack saw his father only once more. Barack was ten years old when his father came to Hawaii to visit for a month at Christmastime. By then, Barack felt as if his father were a stranger. He didn't look the way the young boy had imagined. He was older, thinner, and he had a limp.

One night his father told him to turn off the TV and study. Barack went to his room and slammed the door. Why was this stranger telling him what to do?

But little by little, Barack came to know his father. They went to a jazz concert together. His father visited Barack's school. Many afternoons they lay side by side, reading books. And Barack's father taught his son how to dance, African style. These were memories Barack would always keep.

His father never returned to the United States. Still, he and Barack stayed in touch

through letters. Barack did not visit
Kenya until after college. By that time,
his father had been killed in a car crash.
But later on, Barack wrote a book called
Dreams from My Father. In it, he talked
about his father's powerful influence on
him.

In 1967, Barack's mother married again. Her new husband, Lolo, was from Indonesia. This map shows you where Indonesia is.

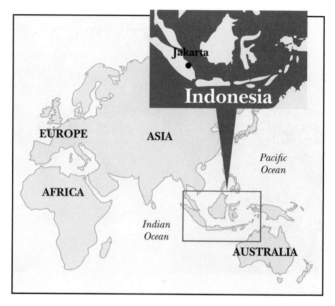

For four years, young Barack lived in a house just outside Jakarta, the capital city. His younger sister, Maya, was born there. Chickens and ducks ran around the backyard. In a fenced-off pond were two baby crocodiles. Barack even had a pet ape. Its name was Tata.

Lolo treated Barack like a son.

One day, after Barack got into a fight with an older boy who had stolen a soccer ball, Lolo brought home two pairs of boxing gloves: a pair for himself and a smaller pair for Barack. Lolo taught Barack how to box so that Barack could stand up for himself.

The city of Jakarta

Barack's class photo in Jakarta at the SDN Menteng School

Barack was smart—very smart. But he didn't always behave in class. He once said, "I was such a terror that my teachers didn't know what to do with me."

Barack's mother worried that the schools in Jakarta were not good enough for her son. She wanted him to have the best education possible.

And she worried about crime in the
crowded city of Jakarta. So she decided
to send Barack to Honolulu, Hawaii, where
her parents—Barack's grandparents—
now lived. An excellent private school
accepted Barack. It was called the
Punahou School. (You pronounce it like
this: PUN-ah-HOW.)

So now Barack was separated from both
his mother and his father. But Barack was
close to his grandparents. He called them
Toot and Gramps. Of course, they were
much older than the parents of the other
kids. And they were white. His "family"
looked very different from other families.

Toot and Gramps didn't have much
money. At Punahou, nearly all the other
kids were rich.

Was there any place where Barack felt like he fit in?

Yes. He learned to play basketball. In fact, Barack was crazy about basketball. He practiced whenever he could. He was good—good enough to be on the Punahou team. But he wasn't great. Part of what he liked so much about basketball was being on a team. It made him feel like he belonged.

In high school, Barack had friends of all races. He was an open-minded guy.

One time, a black friend at Punahou was upset because a white girl in their class wouldn't go on a date with him. He thought she was racist, that she didn't like blacks. But Barack saw it a different way.

He told his friend that lots of girls wanted to date "someone who looks like their daddy, or brother, or whatever, and we ain't it."

Even when he got to college, Barack was still pushing "questions of who I was out of my mind." And after he graduated from Columbia University in New York City, Barack wasn't sure at all what his next step should be. What did he want to do with his life? Where did he want to put down roots?

He walked all around New York City, getting a look at different neighborhoods. He liked the city. But he saw a lot of ill will between black people and white people. Even at Columbia University, Barack was aware of it. In the bathroom stalls of his dorm, nasty remarks were written on the walls. No matter how many times the walls were repainted, new nasty words appeared.

There was one thing that Barack was sure of. He wanted to help people who were struggling; people whose lives were much worse off than his own.

Barack wrote to community centers in cities all over the United States, hoping for a job.

The only reply was from a group working in a poor neighborhood in the South Side of Chicago.

So off he went in 1985. Barack spent
the next three years working in Chicago,
Illinois.

At this time in Illinois, many factories had closed. Many people were out of work. They were desperate. And the government wasn't helping enough.

Barack talked to lots of people. He heard lots of stories. In a housing project, people paid rent for apartments with broken toilets, broken windows, broken heaters. A neighborhood school didn't have enough textbooks for the students. People deserved a decent place to live. Children deserved a good education.

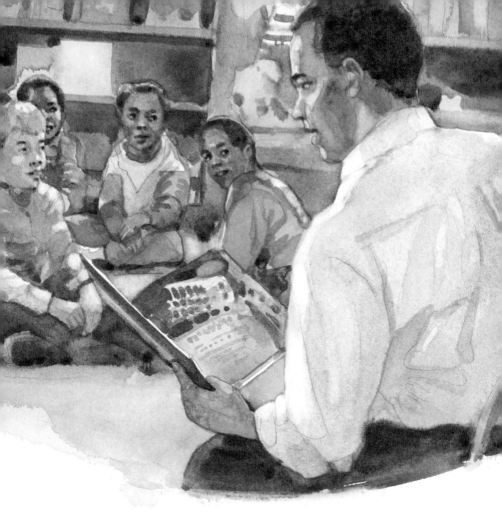

Barack did what he could to fix problems.
But he saw that changing people's lives
meant changing laws—and making new laws
to help the poor. To learn about the law,
Barack needed to go to law school.

Barack entered Harvard Law School, which is right outside Boston, in 1988. Some of the smartest students in the country were his classmates.

That was no problem for Barack. For all three years of law school, he worked harder than ever before. During his last year, he received a great honor: He was chosen as president of the Harvard Law Review. It was the first time at Harvard Law School that an African American had been chosen. There was a newspaper article about Barack in *The New York Times*.

With a degree from Harvard Law, he could have his pick of good jobs at big, famous law firms. After a few years he could become a rich man. But that didn't interest him.

Instead, Barack returned to Chicago. There were two reasons. He had fallen in love with a young woman named Michelle Robinson, who was also a lawyer. They were married in 1992.

Michelle and Barack Obama at their wedding

Barack also wanted to take up where he'd left off three years before— helping the poor. He started to practice civil rights law.

In the United States, people have many civil rights. They have the right to vote, to get a free education, to live anywhere they choose.

But sometimes people are denied their civil rights because of their race or sex. They apply for a job but are turned down because of who they are, not what they can do.

Sometimes nobody will sell them a home in a neighborhood where all the other families are white.

As a lawyer, Barack could help people go to court to fight for their civil rights. He also headed up a drive to get people registered to vote.

An African-American couple looks for a home.

And he taught a class on the U.S. Constitution at the University of Chicago Law School.

The Constitution is the document, written more than two hundred years ago, that explains how the United States federal government works. The laws of the federal government apply to everybody living in the United States.

Each state has its own constitution and government as well. These laws apply only to the people in that state. Barack decided to run for a seat in the state senate of Illinois. He hoped to represent the people who lived on the South Side of Chicago.

It was the first time Barack Obama had ever run for office. And, in 1996, he won! For eight years he served in the state senate. Barack was a Democrat, but during those years he worked well with Republicans. He fought for the rights of prisoners, for better health care, for more schooling for very young children.

Barack is holding Malia. Michelle holds Sasha.

Barack and Michelle now had two
daughters of their own. Malia was born in
1998, and Sasha was born in 2001.

In 2000, Barack ran for the House of Representatives. (The House of Representatives and the U.S. Senate are part of the federal government.) He lost that election. But that did not stop Barack Obama. He remained in the state senate and was so popular with voters that nobody ran against him in 2002.

In 2004, one of the two U.S. Senate seats from Illinois was open. Barack Obama became the Democratic candidate.

As he campaigned throughout his state, people took note of this young, attractive man who was so bright. People marveled at Barack Obama's way of connecting to an audience. Maybe all those years feeling different helped him connect to all different kinds of people. Black and white. Rich and poor. Farmers and factory workers.

Barack gives the keynote speech at the Democratic National Convention on July 27, 2004.

That same year—2004—was also a presidential election year. In Boston in July, the Democrats held their convention. There, they nominated Senator John Kerry of Massachusetts for president. The Democrats hoped Kerry could beat President George W. Bush, a Republican who was running for a second term.

At any presidential convention, one of the most important speeches is the keynote speech. It sums up what the political party stands for and what it hopes to do for the country.

At the 2004 Democratic convention, Barack Obama delivered the keynote speech.

It was seen on TV by millions of Americans. Barack Obama was suddenly a national celebrity.

It was a wonderful speech. It had a message of unity and harmony. Obama said, among many other things, that "People don't expect government to solve all their problems. But they sense, deep in their bones . . . that . . . we can make sure that every child in America has a decent shot at life, and that the doors of opportunity remain open to all."

His wife, Michelle, was there to hear him. Both his daughters were, too. But his mother had died of cancer, so sadly neither of Barack's parents could share this proud moment. Still, he spoke of his family—his mother from Kansas, his father from Kenya—and where he'd grown up. Maybe that is part of Barack

Obama's appeal: It is as if he has a little bit of everybody in him.

John Kerry lost the race for president that November. But Barack Obama was elected to the U.S. Senate. It was only the fifth time in U.S. history that a black man had been elected to the Senate.

The U.S. Senate works out of Washington, D.C., in the great domed Capitol building. So Barack had to divide his time between Washington and his home and family back in Chicago.

Barack is sworn in to the U.S. Senate.

Most newly elected senators don't get
to work on important committees or pass
important laws. But right away Senator
Obama continued to work on all the same
issues that had always been important to
him. From early on, he also spoke out
against the U.S. war in Iraq. Many people all
across the country agreed with what he said.

In February of 2007, Barack Obama
announced that he was running for
president. He was not the first black person
to do so.

Shirley Chisholm

In 1972, Shirley Chisholm, a U.S. congresswoman from New York, and in 1984 and 1988, Jesse Jackson, a famous civil rights leader, tried to win the Democratic nomination for president. But so far, no black leader had become a candidate for president from the Democratic or Republican party.

Jesse Jackson

Many other politicians, besides Barack Obama, hoped to become the Democratic candidate for president in 2008. By early spring the field had narrowed to Barack and Hillary Clinton.

Hillary, the former First Lady, was a senator from New York. She and Barack agreed on many issues. Like Barack, Hillary was hoping to make history. No woman has ever been the candidate for president from a major party.

Hillary Clinton and Barack Obama

Both Hillary and Barack fought hard.
They met in debates. They spoke to huge
crowds of voters in states that have early
contests called primaries and caucuses.

By early June 2008 it was clear. More
Democrats wanted Obama as their
candidate. From then on, Hillary Clinton
worked to help elect the man whom she
had been fighting against.

Some Clinton supporters hoped that Obama might choose Hillary as his running mate. However, in the end Barack picked Senator Joe Biden from Delaware for his vice president. Earlier in the race, Biden had wanted to be the candidate for president. But he dropped out. When Obama asked him to run for vice president, Biden said yes. The photograph below shows Joe and Jill Biden with Michelle and Barack Obama.

Now Democrats all over the country started wearing Obama-Biden buttons. Some buttons were printed with the slogan "Yes We Can." Some said "Change We Can Believe In." Some had a photo of Barack and his wife Michelle and said "America's Next First Family."

The Democrats' convention took place
in Denver in late August. Only four years
earlier, at the last convention, Barack had
been the keynote speaker. Now he was his
party's nominee!

On the last night of the convention, Barack gave his acceptance speech. He decided not to stay inside the convention hall. Instead he spoke to a record crowd of 84,000 people at Mile High Stadium.

Across the country about 38 million people saw this moment in history on their TV sets.

The Republican convention took place in Saint Paul, Minnesota, just a few days later. Senator John McCain of Arizona was their choice for president.

A Vietnam War hero, he spent five and a half terrible years in a prison camp in North Vietnam. Smart, popular, and funny, John McCain was serving his fourth term as a United States senator.

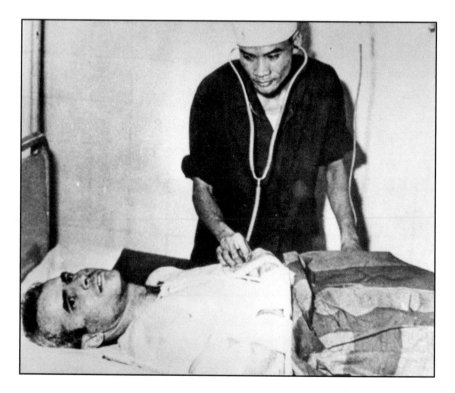

Compared to Barack Obama, he had much more experience in Congress. Like Obama, McCain was known for working with both Republicans and Democrats. In fact, he almost chose Senator Joseph Lieberman as his running mate. Why would this have been so unusual? Joe Lieberman is a Democrat. In fact, in 2000 he had been the Democratic nominee for vice president!

Instead, John McCain picked a newcomer to politics to share his ticket. Her name was Sarah Palin. Since 2006 she had been governor of Alaska. Before that she was the mayor of her hometown.

If the Republicans won, Sarah Palin would also be making history. She would become the first woman to serve as vice president of our country.

It was an exciting campaign. Barack Obama and John McCain crisscrossed the country to tell voters their message.

John McCain's bus was called the Straight Talk Express.

Sometimes Obama would appear in three different states in a single day. Sometimes his family was with him. Most often they weren't. No matter where he was, Obama always called home in the evening. Even if he couldn't be there, he never missed saying good night to Michelle, Malia, and Sasha.

Just about the only time he took off was in October to visit his grandmother. Barack flew to Hawaii. Toot was about to celebrate her 86th birthday. She was frail and sick but as sharp as ever. Sadly it was their last time together. Toot died only two days before the election.

As November 4th drew near, there seemed to be only one thing that nearly everyone in the United States agreed on. The next president was going to take office at a terribly difficult time. The stock market was on a downward spiral. Banks were closing. Hundreds of thousands of people were out of a job. Families were losing their homes because they could no longer pay their monthly mortgage bill. People with homes worried about heating costs with gas prices so high.

The war in Iraq was in its fifth year. More than four thousand U.S. soldiers had died in battle. And still there was no set plan for ending the war.

There had been a Republican president in the White House—George W. Bush—for the past eight years. More and more people thought that it was time for a change.

Malia Obama and her younger sister Sasha appear with their parents and the Bidens at the Democratic National Convention.

On November 4, 2008, people in all
fifty states went to the polls. More than
one-hundred-and-twenty-five million
votes were cast. A record number of
young people turned out. Many were
voting for president for the very first

time. Almost three-quarters of them voted for Obama.

People of color—African Americans, Hispanics, and Asians—voted for Barack Obama in great numbers. So did white voters. Obama beat McCain by more than eight million votes!

On January 20, 2009, in Washington, D.C., Barack Obama became the 44th president of the United States.

In his famous keynote speech in 2004, he talked about people's hopes, and also "the hope of a skinny kid with a funny name." He was talking about himself. He said he always believed America had a place for him. He was right. And that is something we can all take pride in. Yes we can.